Friendship Bracelets

Published by
Mud Puddle Books, Inc.
54 W. 21st Street
Suite 601
New York, NY 10010 USA

info@mudpuddlebooks.com

HINKLER
BOOKS

Hinkler Books Pty Ltd
17 – 23 Redwood Drive
Dingley Victoria 3172 Australia
www.hinklerbooks.com

© Hinkler Books Pty Ltd 2004

Written by: Liz Ungar, Clare Mayhew and Heather Hammonds
Edited by: Heather Hammonds
Design and illustrations by: Monitor Graphics

ISBN: 1-59412-036-6

Printed and bound in China

Contents

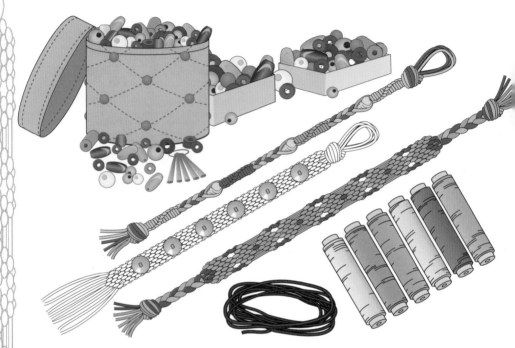

Our Friends

Where would we be without friends? Friends are very important people in our lives, and they come in all shapes and sizes. They may be people, pets, or even your favorite teddy bear. A person can have many friends, or perhaps, just a few very special ones. Either way, it's all good!

A friend can be someone you have known for a long time, or even someone you have just met. Someone you go to school with, a family member such as your cousin, or even a neighbor. A friend is someone you can have fun with, someone who you can rely on and trust, and someone you can share your important secrets with. Most of all, a friend is someone who will stand by you through good times and bad times.

Friendship Bracelet Origins

It's great to give your friends a present, to show them that you care. You can do this by making them a beautiful friendship bracelet. Friendship bracelets are a well- known symbol of friendship. Each bracelet is as individual as the person who made it, and the person who is wearing it. When you are wearing a friendship bracelet, everyone knows that you have a good friend. Sometimes, friends even make each other matching identical friendship bracelets.

Friendship bracelets can be made from many different materials such as cotton thread, colorful cord, string or leather. They are often decorated with beads or other small items of jewelry. There is a wide range of suitable craft materials available today, to make beautiful bracelets.

Superstition has it that when a person gives a friendship bracelet to a special friend, their friendship will last as long as the bracelet stays on that person. If the friendship bracelet is somehow lost or ruined it's

okay, just as long as the bracelet has not been cut. After all, it's easy to make another one!

Friendship bracelets are made through weaving, braiding or knotting threads, or other materials. Weaving, braiding and knotting are art forms that have been practiced for many thousands of years, all around the world. Ancient people wove materials into clothing, using simple hand looms. They wove baskets from grasses and reeds, too.

Leather was braided and knotted to make belts and other useful items. And clothing and homes were decorated with woven, braided and knotted items.

People in central and southern parts of America were expert at making jewelry by weaving, braiding and knotting threads. Some of their handiwork can be seen in museums today. In ancient Britain and Europe, people made beautiful clothing that was decorated with woven, knotted and braided patterns. They even decorated metalwork such as sword handles and belt buckles with woven patterns.

Today, the art of making jewelry by weaving, braiding and knotting is just as popular as ever.

Getting Started

To make your first friendship bracelets, you need a few basic things to get you started. We've provided you with some gorgeous threads in ten different colors, and a small packet of different colored beads. You'll be able to make some beautiful gifts for your friends with these!

YOU WILL ALSO NEED:

- SCISSORS, TO CUT THE THREADS WITH
- A CLIPBOARD, HARD COVER BOOK OR SMALL SQUARE PIECE OF BOARD, TO ATTACH THE BRACELET TO WHILE YOU ARE MAKING IT
- A RULER OR TAPE MEASURE, TO MEASURE THE THREADS
- STICKY TAPE – HANDY TO HELP KEEP THREADS SEPARATE
- A FLAT, CLEAN PLACE TO WORK, SUCH AS A KITCHEN TABLE

Getting Started

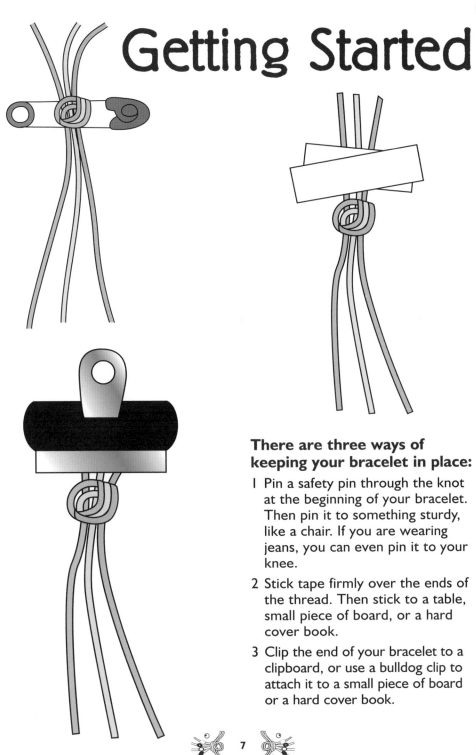

There are three ways of keeping your bracelet in place:

1 Pin a safety pin through the knot at the beginning of your bracelet. Then pin it to something sturdy, like a chair. If you are wearing jeans, you can even pin it to your knee.

2 Stick tape firmly over the ends of the thread. Then stick to a table, small piece of board, or a hard cover book.

3 Clip the end of your bracelet to a clipboard, or use a bulldog clip to attach it to a small piece of board or a hard cover book.

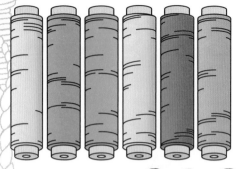

Threads....

After you've become an expert at making friendship bracelets with the threads and beads we've provided, you might like to try using some other types of craft materials. You will be able to buy them at your nearest craft store, or department store.

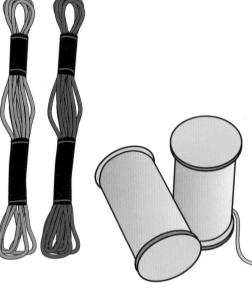

Sewing or Embroidery Thread

Sewing thread or machine embroidery thread is the best type of material to begin making friendship bracelets with. Thread can be purchased in all sorts of colors. You can buy cotton thread, or thread made from fibers such as polyester. You can also buy sparkly thread, and even glow-in-the-dark thread!

Embroidery Floss

Embroidery floss, also called embroidery silk, is a thicker type of thread that is used for hand embroidery. It is perfect for making thicker bracelets and comes in a huge range of bright colors.

Upholstery Thread

Upholstery thread is a type of heavy duty sewing thread that is perfect for making friendship bracelets, as it's so hard to break. It is often used for sewing projects such as making teddy bears, because it is so strong. It comes in many colors and is a good thread to use when you are including beads in your friendship bracelets.

....and Things

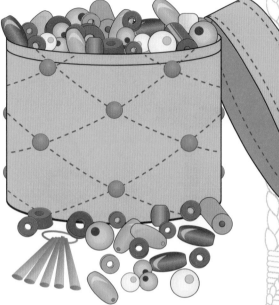

Silky Cord / Elastic Cord

For a chunkier bracelet, you might like to try some of the sturdy cords available today. They come in black and white, but can also be found in a range of colors.

Gold and silver cord looks especially good when you and your friends are at a party or other special occasion.

Leather Cord

You can make beautiful, earthy friendship bracelets that last for many months with thin strips of leather cord. Leather cord is easy to work with. Some types have a shiny side and a dull side. Another type, called suede cord, has a softer feel and look.

Beads

Beads can add that special touch to a friendship bracelet. They come in a variety of sizes and colors, from tiny pony beads to bigger novelty beads, in lots of different shapes. You can buy beads that look like jewels, and even beads that glow in the dark.

TIP!

Start your own collection of friendship bracelet materials. Then you'll always have some on hand to make that special person the bracelet that's just right for them.

Basic Knots: Left Hand

You can use several different types of knots, braids and weaving techniques to make friendship bracelets. However, to start off with, all you need to know is how to tie a left and right version of one simple knot.

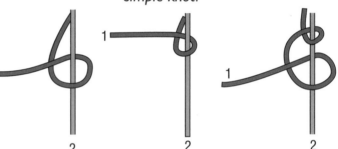

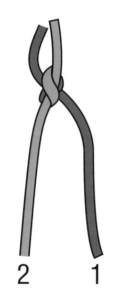

1 Take two different colored threads and tie them together. Then secure them to a clipboard (or use one of the other techniques shown on Page 7).

2 Now the threads should be hanging side by side. Call the left hand thread, Thread 1. Call the right hand thread, Thread 2.

3 Hold Thread 2 (right hand thread) firmly, and tie Thread 1 (left hand thread) around it.

4 Pull Thread 1 tight towards the left.

5 Repeat steps 3 and 4, to give you a double knot. This is how your left hand knot should look.

Basic Knots: Right Hand

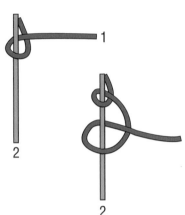

1 Take two different colored threads and tie them together. Then secure them to a clipboard (or use one of the other techniques shown on Page 7).

2 Now the threads should be hanging side by side. Call the left hand thread, Thread 1. Call the right hand thread, Thread 2.

3 Hold Thread 1 (left hand thread) firmly, and tie Thread 2 (right hand thread) around it.

4 Pull Thread 2 tight towards the right.

5 Repeat steps 3 and 4, to give you a double knot. This is how your right hand knot should look.

TIP!

Try using thicker string or wool when learning how to tie knots. This will make it easier for you to see if you are tying the knots correctly.

11

Popular Patterns

In this book, we have featured some of the most popular friendship bracelet patterns around today. Work your way through the patterns, starting with the easiest. Before you know it you'll be an expert. Then you can try inventing your own patterns!

Stripy, Stripy

A beautiful, basic first pattern.

Twin Ties

A chunky pattern that looks great when made with embroidery floss.

Simple Braids

Ever braided hair? This pattern uses the same technique, with great results.

Twister

A lovely pattern of twists and braids.

Beaded Braids

A simple, elegant pattern that is a perfect first beading project.

Popular Patterns

Friendship Arrows

A more advanced project with bold, bright arrows.

Arrows and Twists

An exotic combination pattern that your friends will love.

Beaded Arrows

A stunning advanced project that you'll want to keep yourself.

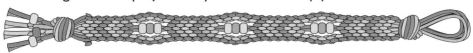

Something Fishy

Plaits and knots make this pattern really stand out.

TIP!

You can create many combinations of these friendship bracelet patterns. Some we feature in this booklet. Others you can design yourself.

First Projects

Okay, it's time to get down to creating some beautiful bracelets! Start off with these super first projects.

Stripy, Stripy

This whole bracelet is made with the basic left hand knot, making it ideal for your very first project. Why not make one for yourself, to start off with?

YOU WILL NEED:

- FOUR DIFFERENT COLORED THREADS OF YOUR CHOICE
- TAPE MEASURE
- SCISSORS
- CLIPBOARD, OR OTHER METHOD OF SECURING YOUR THREADS FROM PAGE 7

1 Cut each of the four threads about 24 in. (61 cm) long.

2 Tie a knot about 2 in. (5 cm) from the top of the threads.

3 Now clip the threads to the clipboard, or use one of the other methods on Page 7 to keep them firmly in place. Separate the threads, to make them easier to work with.

4 Start knotting with Thread 1 (remember, that's the left hand thread). Tie a left hand knot over Thread 2. Hold Thread 2

1 2 3 4

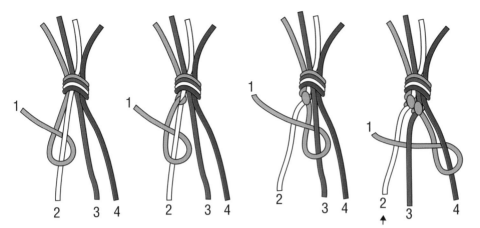

This is the string you'll
be working with next.

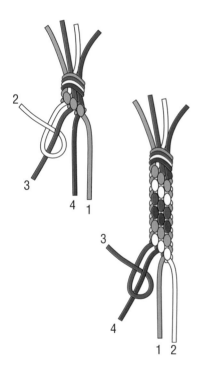

firmly and pull Thread 1 tightly towards
the left. Now repeat Step 1 again to
make a double knot.

5 Now take Thread 1 and tie double knots
around Threads 3 and 4, moving from
left to right.

6 Keep Thread 1 over to the right hand
side. Using Thread 2, tie double knots
across all the different threads from left
to right, until you have completed
another row.

7 Continue tying knots until the bracelet is
as long as you like, then tie a knot and
cut the threads. Leave about 4 in. (10
cm), so that you can tie the bracelet
around your friend's wrist.

TIP!

Stripy, Stripy is made with four colored
threads. However, you can use as many
threads as you like to make the bracelet
wider.

Twin Ties

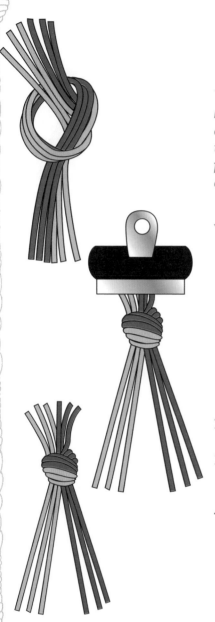

This is one of the easiest bracelets to make and you can create a new one very quickly. This makes it perfect for those times when your friend loses their friendship bracelet and needs another as soon as possible.

YOU WILL NEED:

- SIX THREADS IN TWO DIFFERENT COLORS OF YOUR CHOICE
- TAPE MEASURE
- SCISSORS
- CLIPBOARD, OR OTHER METHOD OF SECURING YOUR THREADS FROM PAGE 7

1 Cut each thread about 24 in. (61 cm) long.

2 Tie a knot about 2 in. (5 cm) from the top of the threads.

3 Now clip the threads to the clipboard, or use one of the other methods on Page 7 to keep them firmly in place.

4 Separate the threads, one color to the left and one color to the right, to make two bunches of threads – three threads in each bunch.

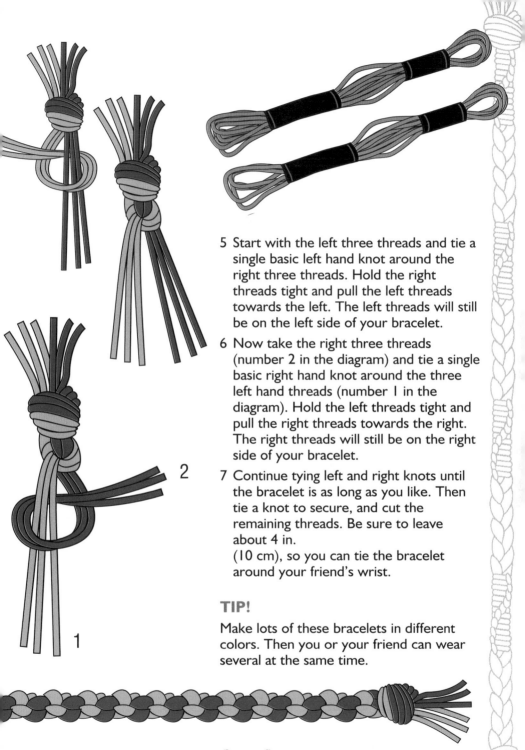

5 Start with the left three threads and tie a single basic left hand knot around the right three threads. Hold the right threads tight and pull the left threads towards the left. The left threads will still be on the left side of your bracelet.

6 Now take the right three threads (number 2 in the diagram) and tie a single basic right hand knot around the three left hand threads (number 1 in the diagram). Hold the left threads tight and pull the right threads towards the right. The right threads will still be on the right side of your bracelet.

7 Continue tying left and right knots until the bracelet is as long as you like. Then tie a knot to secure, and cut the remaining threads. Be sure to leave about 4 in. (10 cm), so you can tie the bracelet around your friend's wrist.

TIP!

Make lots of these bracelets in different colors. Then you or your friend can wear several at the same time.

Simple Braids

Braiding is one of the oldest forms of weaving. It is used to create jewelry, rugs and to braid hair. Try this first simple but beautiful design. We know you'll love it!

YOU WILL NEED:

- THREE DIFFERENT COLORED THREADS – FIVE THREADS OF EACH COLOR
- TAPE MEASURE
- SCISSORS
- CLIPBOARD, OR OTHER METHOD OF SECURING YOUR THREADS FROM PAGE 7

1 Cut each thread about 24 in. (61 cm) long.

2 Tie a knot about 2 in. (5 cm) from the top of the threads.

3 Now clip the threads to the clipboard, or use one of the other methods on Page 7 to keep them firmly in place.

4 Separate the threads into three different bunches, so you have five threads of the same color in each bunch. Call them Bunch 1, Bunch 2, and Bunch 3 (see diagram). Because you are using so many threads, be careful they don't get tangled.

Bunch 1   Bunch 2   Bunch 3

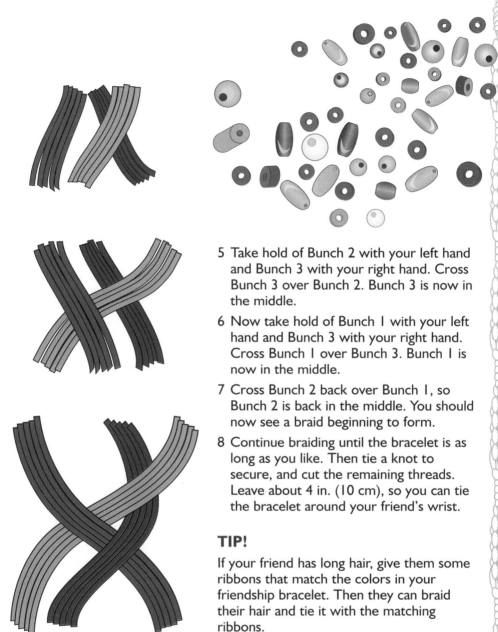

5 Take hold of Bunch 2 with your left hand and Bunch 3 with your right hand. Cross Bunch 3 over Bunch 2. Bunch 3 is now in the middle.

6 Now take hold of Bunch 1 with your left hand and Bunch 3 with your right hand. Cross Bunch 1 over Bunch 3. Bunch 1 is now in the middle.

7 Cross Bunch 2 back over Bunch 1, so Bunch 2 is back in the middle. You should now see a braid beginning to form.

8 Continue braiding until the bracelet is as long as you like. Then tie a knot to secure, and cut the remaining threads. Leave about 4 in. (10 cm), so you can tie the bracelet around your friend's wrist.

TIP!

If your friend has long hair, give them some ribbons that match the colors in your friendship bracelet. Then they can braid their hair and tie it with the matching ribbons.

Twister

This unique friendship bracelet uses braiding and knotting techniques to create a look that your friends will love. It's quick, easy and fun to make. Once you have mastered it, try using more threads to make an even thicker bracelet!

1

YOU WILL NEED:

- SIX THREADS IN THREE COLORS OF YOUR CHOICE (TWO OF EACH COLOR)
- TAPE MEASURE
- SCISSORS
- CLIPBOARD, OR OTHER METHOD OF SECURING YOUR THREADS FROM PAGE 7

1 Cut each thread about 24 in. (61 cm) long. Then tie a knot about 2 in. (5 cm) from the top of the threads.

2 Clip the threads to the clipboard, or use one of the other methods on Page 7 to keep them firmly in place.

3 Now collect all the threads together in a bunch, leaving one thread out

4 Tie a basic left hand knot with the single Thread 1, around the bunch. Repeat this ten times, making sure the knots are pulled tight towards the left each time.

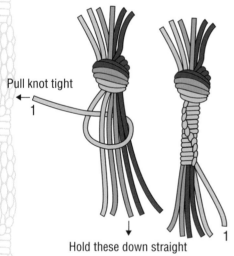

Pull knot tight
1

Hold these down straight
1

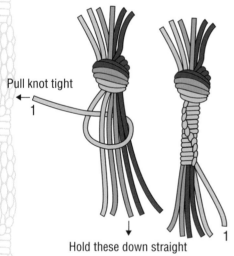

knotted
part

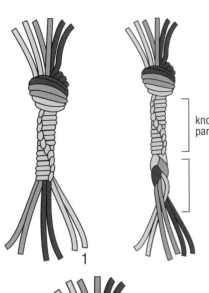

1

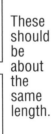

These
should
be
about
the
same
length.

Leave
one
out.

5 Separate the threads into three different bunches, one of each of the three colors. Now you have two threads of the same color in each bunch.

6 Braid the three bunches using the technique shown in the previous pattern on Page 18, until the braided part of the bracelet is as long as the knotted part.

7 Now collect all the threads together again. Leave one thread out, making sure it is a different color to the first thread used for knotting, in Step 3. This thread will now be called Thread 1.

8 Repeat Steps 4-7 until the bracelet is as long as you like. Then tie a knot to secure and cut the remaining threads, leaving about 4 in. (10 cm), so you can tie the bracelet around your friend's wrist.

TIP!

Practice makes perfect! The more bracelets you make, the better at braiding and knotting you'll become.

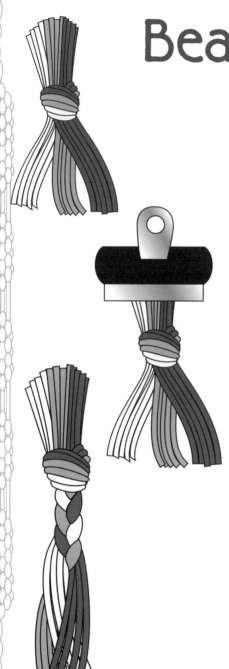

Beaded Braids

Now you've made both braided and knotted friendship bracelets, it's time to try something a little harder. Add some beads to a braided bracelet, to add glitter and style to your special friend's gift!

YOU WILL NEED:

- THREE DIFFERENT COLORED THREADS – FOUR THREADS OF EACH COLOR
- SMALL BEADS – EITHER THE ONES IN THIS PACK OR OTHERS YOU HAVE CHOSEN
- TAPE MEASURE
- SCISSORS
- CLIPBOARD, OR OTHER METHOD OF SECURING YOUR THREADS FROM PAGE 7

1 Cut each thread about 30 in. (76 cm) long. Then tie a knot about 4 in. (10 cm) from the top of the threads.

2 Now clip the threads to the clipboard, or use one of the other methods on Page 7 to keep them firmly in place.

3 Separate the threads into three different bunches, so you have four threads of the same color in each bunch. Call them Bunch 1, Bunch 2, and Bunch 3 (see diagram). Because you are using so many threads, be careful they don't get tangled.

4 Using the technique shown for Simple Braids on Page 18, begin braiding. To start off with just do two braids, as shown here.

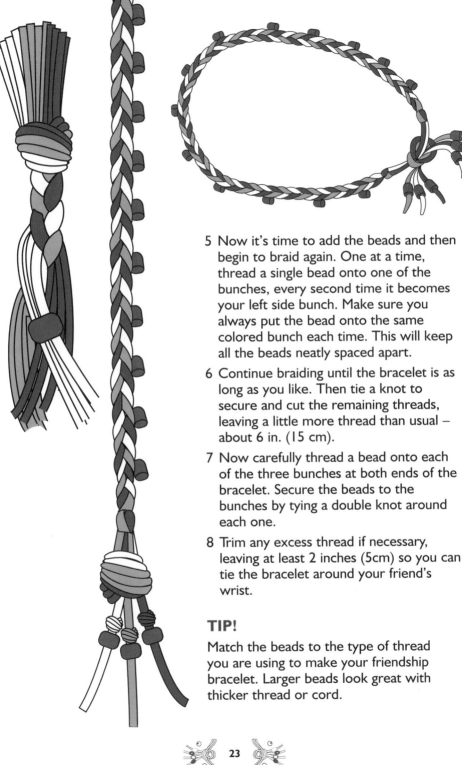

5 Now it's time to add the beads and then begin to braid again. One at a time, thread a single bead onto one of the bunches, every second time it becomes your left side bunch. Make sure you always put the bead onto the same colored bunch each time. This will keep all the beads neatly spaced apart.

6 Continue braiding until the bracelet is as long as you like. Then tie a knot to secure and cut the remaining threads, leaving a little more thread than usual – about 6 in. (15 cm).

7 Now carefully thread a bead onto each of the three bunches at both ends of the bracelet. Secure the beads to the bunches by tying a double knot around each one.

8 Trim any excess thread if necessary, leaving at least 2 inches (5cm) so you can tie the bracelet around your friend's wrist.

TIP!

Match the beads to the type of thread you are using to make your friendship bracelet. Larger beads look great with thicker thread or cord.

Advanced Projects

Once you've learned how to make the friendship bracelets on the previous pages, try some of the following gorgeous patterns.

Friendship Arrows

The bright and colorful arrows on this bracelet are sure to go straight to your best friend's heart! To create it, you'll be using both basic left hand and right hand knots.

YOU WILL NEED:

- FOUR DIFFERENT COLORED THREADS OF YOUR CHOICE
- TAPE MEASURE
- SCISSORS
- CLIPBOARD, OR OTHER METHOD OF SECURING YOUR THREADS FROM PAGE 7

1 1 3 3 4 4 2 2

1 2 3 4   4 3 2 1

1 Cut each thread about 54 in. (137 cm) long.

2 Carefully fold the threads in half. Then tie a knot about 2 in. (5 cm) from the top of the threads, making a loop. Now you will have eight threads – two of each color.

3 Clip the threads to the clipboard, or use one of the other methods on Page 7 to keep them firmly in place. Separate the threads and arrange them in the order shown.

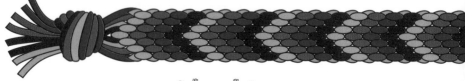

2 3 4   4 3 2 1   2 3 4 1 4 3   2 3 4 1 1 4 3 2   2 3 4 1 1 4 3 2

4 Using the first thread (Thread 1) on the left side, tie a basic left hand knot around Threads 2, 3 and 4, moving from left to right. Stop in the middle. Remember to always use double knots.

5 Now take the first thread (Thread 1) on the right side and again move towards the middle, tying basic right hand double knots around Threads 2, 3 and 4. Move from right to left, and stop in the middle.

6 Tie the two middle Thread 1s together, using a basic right hand knot. Make sure you pull the knot tight towards the right.

7 Your bracelet should now look like the diagram above right, with the two Thread 1s knotted in the middle. Repeat Steps 4-6, beginning with the outside threads each time and working towards the middle.

8 When your bracelet is at the desired length, tie a knot and cut the threads, leaving about 4 in. (10 cm) to tie the bracelet around your friend's wrist. Now find a friend to give it to!

TIP!

Try using a small piece of tape to stick the threads on the side you aren't working on to your clipboard or book. This will help stop them from getting tangled.

Arrows and Twists

Make sure you've practiced the friendship arrow bracelet on Page 24 before you try this one. Its beautiful pattern is harder to create, but it is well worth the effort. All your friends will want you to make one for them, when they see it!

1 2 3 4   4 3 2 1

YOU WILL NEED:

- FOUR DIFFERENT COLORED THREADS OF YOUR CHOICE
- TAPE MEASURE
- SCISSORS
- CLIPBOARD, OR OTHER METHOD OF SECURING YOUR THREADS FROM PAGE 7

1 Cut each thread about 60 in. (152 cm) long.

2 Carefully fold the threads in half. Then tie a knot about 2 in. (5 cm) from the top of the threads, making a loop. Now you will have eight threads – two of each color.

3 Clip the threads to the clipboard, or use one of the other methods on Page 7 to keep them firmly in place. Separate the threads and arrange them in the order shown.

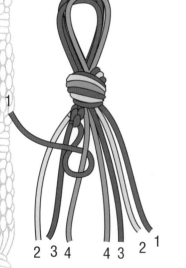

2 3 4   4 3 2 1

2 3 4 1 4 3 2 1

↑
This is the string you'll
be working with next.

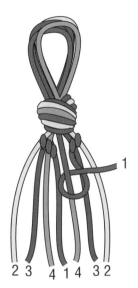

1

2 3 4 1 4 3 2

2 3 4 1 1 4 3 2

2 3 4 1 1 4 3 2

4 Now make a single arrow, using the same method you used for the Friendship Arrows bracelet. Using Thread 1 on the left side, tie a basic left hand knot around Threads 2, 3 and 4, moving from left to right. Stop in the middle. Remember to always use double knots.

5 Now take Thread 1 on the right side and again move towards the middle, tying basic right hand double knots around Threads 2,3 and 4. Move from right to left, and stop in the middle.

6 Tie the two middle Thread 1s together, using a basic right hand knot. Make sure you pull the knot tight towards the right. Your bracelet should now look like the diagram below left, with the two Thread 1s knotted in the middle.

TIP!

Contrasting light and dark thread colors look great on this type of bracelet. For example, two shades of brown thread and two shades of gold thread.

Arrows and Twists (continued)

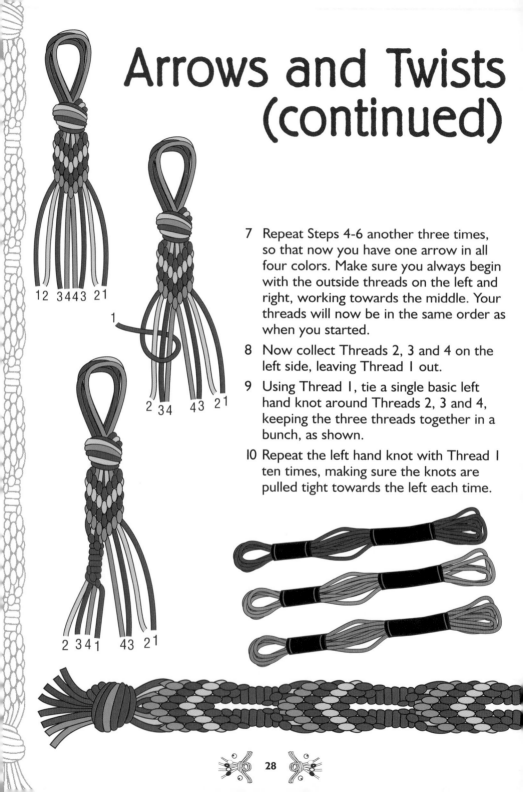

12 3443 21

1

2 34   43 21

2 341   43 21

7 Repeat Steps 4-6 another three times, so that now you have one arrow in all four colors. Make sure you always begin with the outside threads on the left and right, working towards the middle. Your threads will now be in the same order as when you started.

8 Now collect Threads 2, 3 and 4 on the left side, leaving Thread 1 out.

9 Using Thread 1, tie a single basic left hand knot around Threads 2, 3 and 4, keeping the three threads together in a bunch, as shown.

10 Repeat the left hand knot with Thread 1 ten times, making sure the knots are pulled tight towards the left each time.

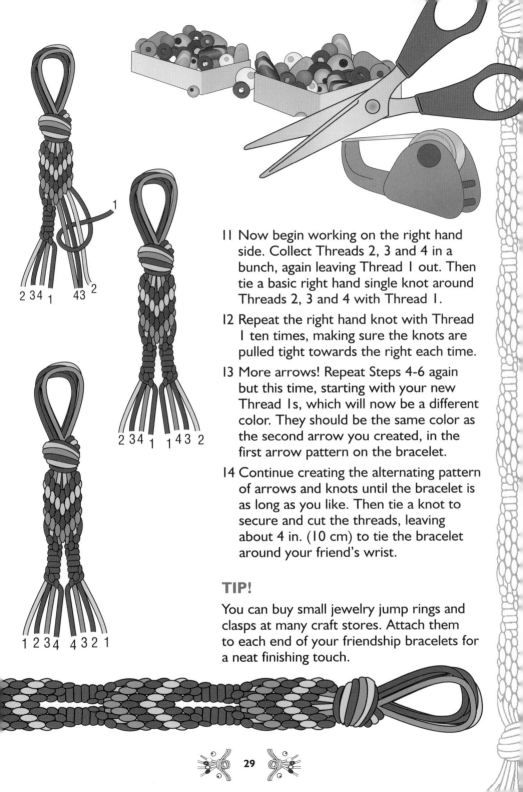

11 Now begin working on the right hand side. Collect Threads 2, 3 and 4 in a bunch, again leaving Thread 1 out. Then tie a basic right hand single knot around Threads 2, 3 and 4 with Thread 1.

12 Repeat the right hand knot with Thread 1 ten times, making sure the knots are pulled tight towards the right each time.

13 More arrows! Repeat Steps 4-6 again but this time, starting with your new Thread 1s, which will now be a different color. They should be the same color as the second arrow you created, in the first arrow pattern on the bracelet.

14 Continue creating the alternating pattern of arrows and knots until the bracelet is as long as you like. Then tie a knot to secure and cut the threads, leaving about 4 in. (10 cm) to tie the bracelet around your friend's wrist.

TIP!

You can buy small jewelry jump rings and clasps at many craft stores. Attach them to each end of your friendship bracelets for a neat finishing touch.

Beaded Arrows

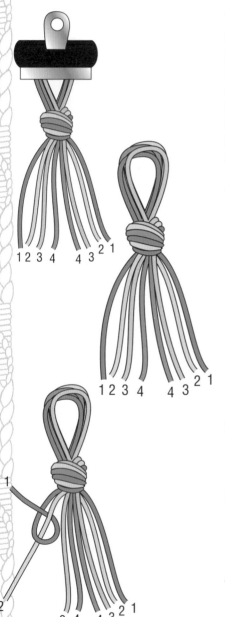

1 2 3 4   4 3 ² ¹

1 2 3 4   4 3 ² ¹

1

2

3 4   4 3 ² ¹

This is one of the most difficult friendship bracelet patterns in this book, but if you've practiced making the bracelets on the earlier pages, you should be ready for it! If you don't get the pattern right the first time, just try again. It's well worth it because the finished bracelet is so beautiful that you'll have to make two – one for your friend and one for yourself!

YOU WILL NEED:

- FOUR DIFFERENT COLORED THREADS OF YOUR CHOICE
- SMALL BEADS – EITHER ONES FROM THIS PACK OR OTHERS YOU HAVE CHOSEN
- TAPE MEASURE
- SCISSORS
- CLIPBOARD, OR OTHER METHOD OF SECURING YOUR THREADS FROM PAGE 7

1 Cut each thread about 60 in. (152 cm) long.

2 Carefully fold the threads in half. Then tie a knot about 2 in. (5 cm) from the top of the threads, making a loop. Now you will have eight threads – two of each color.

3 Clip the threads to the clipboard, or use one of the other methods on Page 7 to keep them firmly in place. Separate the threads and arrange them in the order shown.

4 Start with the first Thread 1, the outside thread on the left. Tie a single basic left hand knot onto Thread 2. Don't do a double knot, as you usually would.

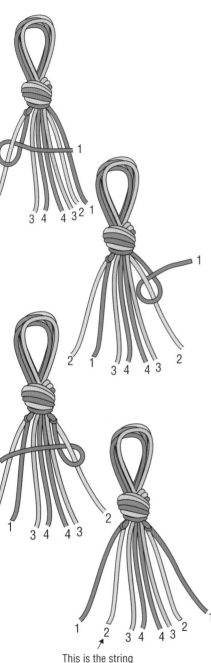

This is the string you'll be using next.

5 Now tie another single knot with the same Thread 1. This time, tie a single basic right hand knot around Thread 2. Make sure you pull the knots tight each time. The threads will now be back in the same order as when you began. This completes the first knots on what will become the left border of the bracelet pattern.

6 Using the outside thread on the right, Thread 1, tie a single basic right hand knot around Thread 2. Again, don't do a double knot as you usually would.

7 Now tie another single knot with the same Thread 1. This time, tie a single basic left hand knot around Thread 2. Once more, make sure you pull the knots tight each time. The threads will now be back in their original order. This completes the first knots on what will become the right border of this bracelet pattern.

TIP!

If you are having trouble creating this bracelet, try practicing Steps 4-7 several times first, before moving on to Step 8.

  31

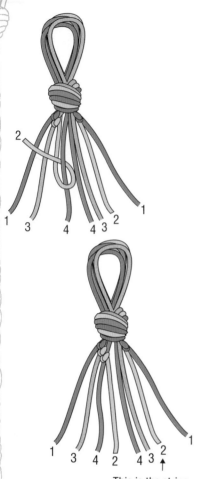

Beaded Arrows (continued)

8 Put both left and right outside threads out of the way. You will not need them again for a few steps. For the moment, you will only be usingThreads 2, 3 and 4 on both sides.

9 Tie basic left hand double knots with the left Thread 2, around Threads 3 and 4, moving towards the middle.

10 Now tie basic right hand double knots with the right Thread 2, around Threads 3 and 4. Again, work towards the middle.

11 Tie both Threads 2 together, using a basic double right hand knot, to end up like this.

This is the string you'll be using next.

1 2 3 4 4   3 2 1   1 2 3 4 4   3 2 1

1

2   3 4 4   3 2 1

1

1 2 3 4 4 3   2

12 Now repeat Steps 4-11 until you have made six bordered arrows.

13 Choose two or three beads and carefully thread them onto the two middle threads, Threads 4.

14 You will now be working with one side of the bracelet at a time, starting with the left side. Again, using Thread 1 (the thread which you put to the side), tie a single basic left hand knot around Thread 2.

15 Now tie a basic right hand knot using the same threads, to make another border. This is the same procedure as you used in Steps 4 and 5.

TIP!

If you are having trouble remembering which colored thread is which number, simply write it down on a piece of paper beside you, before you begin making a bracelet.

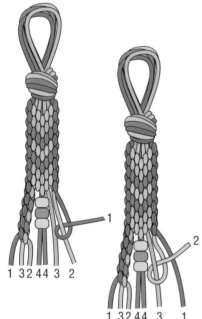

Beaded Arrows (continued)

16 Using Thread 2, tie a basic left hand double knot around Thread 3, pulling Thread 2 towards the left and keeping Thread 3 nice and tight. Repeat Steps 14, 15 and 16 until the borders of the bracelet are as long as the beads.

17 Now you need to work on the right hand side of the bracelet. Using Thread 1 on the right side, tie a single basic right hand knot around Thread 2. Then tie a basic left hand knot, using the same threads. This will make another border.

18 Using Thread 2 on the right side, tie a basic right hand double knot around Thread 3, pulling Thread 2 towards the right and keeping Thread 3 nice and tight.

19 Repeat Steps 17 and 18 until the right hand border of the bracelet is as long as the left hand side.

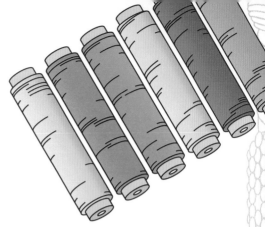

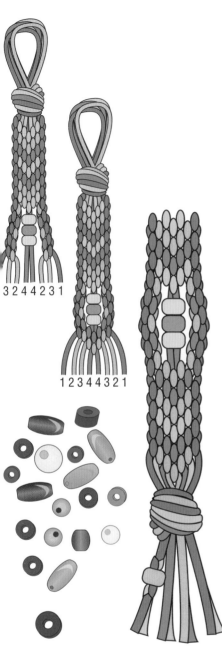

3 2 4 4 2 3 1

1 2 3 4 4 3 2 1

20 Congratulations, you have completed the first part of the bracelet! It only gets easier from here. Now you need to begin again and repeat Steps 4 to 19, to complete the next part of your bracelet.

21 Continue this pattern until the bracelet is as long as you like (usually four to six sets of Steps 4 to 19). Then tie a knot, to secure.

22 As an extra decoration, take four beads and carefully thread a bead on two strands of each color, as shown. Secure each bead tightly with a double knot.

23 Cut excess threads, leaving about 4 in. (10 cm) so you can tie the bracelet around your friend's wrist. Congratulations, you've finished!

TIP!

The best beads to use for this pattern are very small 'pony beads'. They are available at most craft stores.

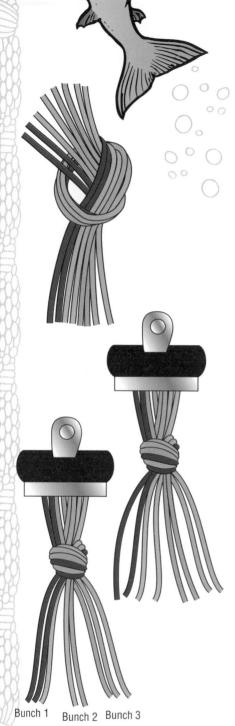

Something Fishy

Okay, if you've successfully completed the Beaded Arrows project you're ready to try the most difficult project in this book. This bracelet is made up of arrows that not only point down, as you have previously made, but also point up. As you make this bracelet, you will notice a beautiful fish-like pattern forming. The perfect bracelet to give your best friend after a trip to the beach!

YOU WILL NEED:

- FOUR DIFFERENT COLORED THREADS OF YOUR CHOICE
- TAPE MEASURE
- SCISSORS
- CLIPBOARD, OR OTHER METHOD OF SECURING YOUR THREADS FROM PAGE 7
- STICKY TAPE

1 Cut two strands of each color thread, about 60 in. (152 cm) long. You will now have eight threads.

2 Tie a knot about 2 in. (5 cm) from the top of all the threads. Now you will have eight threads – two of each color.

3 Clip the threads to the clipboard, or use one of the other methods on Page 7 to keep them firmly in place. Separate the eight threads into three different bunches as shown – two outside bunches of three threads and a middle bunch of two threads.

Bunch 1   Bunch 2   Bunch 3

1 2 3 4   4 3 2 1   2 3   4   4 3 2 1   2 3 4 1   4 3   2

1   1

2 3 4 1   1 4 3 2

1
2
  3 4 4 3

1
2

4 Use the braiding technique we showed you in the Simple Braids pattern on Page 18, to braid the threads for 2 in. (5 cm). Then secure the braids with a small piece of tape, as shown.

5 Next you need to make an arrow, using the technique we showed in Friendship Arrows pattern on Page 24. Take the left hand Thread 1 and, using a basic left hand knot, tie double knots around Threads 2,3 and 4, moving into the middle from left to right.

6 Now take Thread 1 on the right hand side and again work towards the middle, tying double knots around Threads 2, 3 and 4.

7 Using a basic right hand knot, tie the two Thread 1s together. Make sure you pull the knot tight towards the right. Repeat Steps 5-6 again, until you have four arrows – one of each color.

TIP!

Try making this pattern using threads that are different shades of blue and green to give it that seaside feel.

Something Fishy (continued)

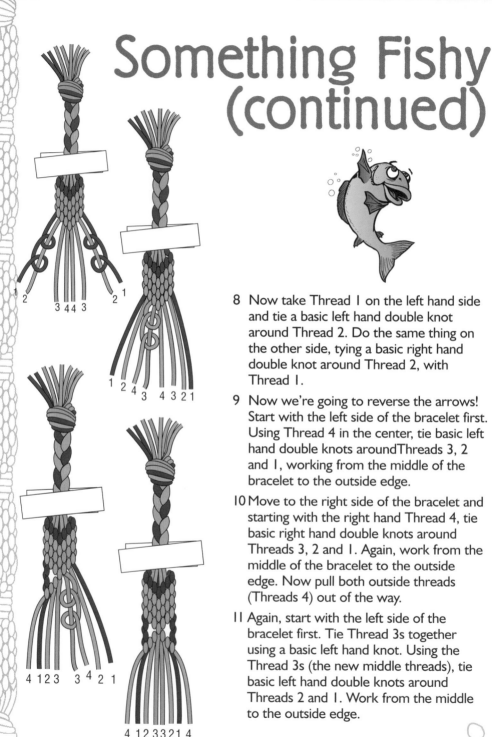

8 Now take Thread 1 on the left hand side and tie a basic left hand double knot around Thread 2. Do the same thing on the other side, tying a basic right hand double knot around Thread 2, with Thread 1.

9 Now we're going to reverse the arrows! Start with the left side of the bracelet first. Using Thread 4 in the center, tie basic left hand double knots around Threads 3, 2 and 1, working from the middle of the bracelet to the outside edge.

10 Move to the right side of the bracelet and starting with the right hand Thread 4, tie basic right hand double knots around Threads 3, 2 and 1. Again, work from the middle of the bracelet to the outside edge. Now pull both outside threads (Threads 4) out of the way.

11 Again, start with the left side of the bracelet first. Tie Thread 3s together using a basic left hand knot. Using the Thread 3s (the new middle threads), tie basic left hand double knots around Threads 2 and 1. Work from the middle to the outside edge.

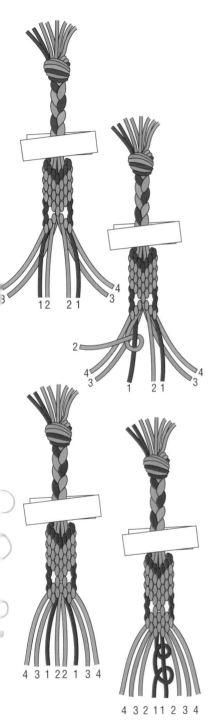

12 Now move to the right side of the bracelet. Use the right hand Thread 3 (middle thread) to tie basic right hand double knots around Threads 2 and 1. Put both outside threads (Threads 3) out of the way. You will now have two threads on each side out of the way.

13 Once again, you need to repeat the same thing with Thread 2. Start with the left side of the bracelet first. Tie Thread 2 (the new middle thread) around Thread 1, using a basic left hand double knot, working from the middle.

14 Do the same on the other side, tying a basic right hand double knot around the right Thread 2, with Thread 1. Then put both Threads 2 out of the way.

15 At this point you will have two threads remaining in the middle – the two Threads 1. Tie the right Thread 1 around the left Thread 1 using a basic right hand double knot. This makes the centre of the fish.

TIP!

It helps to shine a bright light on your bracelet when you are working, especially if you are making a more complicated pattern or using very fine threads. Try putting a desk lamp on your work table!

Something Fishy (continued)

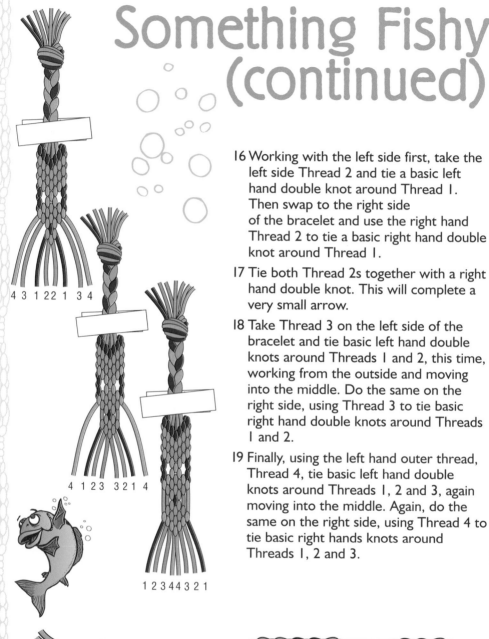

4 3 1 22 1 3 4

4 1 23 3 21 4

1 2 3 44 3 2 1

16 Working with the left side first, take the left side Thread 2 and tie a basic left hand double knot around Thread 1. Then swap to the right side of the bracelet and use the right hand Thread 2 to tie a basic right hand double knot around Thread 1.

17 Tie both Thread 2s together with a right hand double knot. This will complete a very small arrow.

18 Take Thread 3 on the left side of the bracelet and tie basic left hand double knots around Threads 1 and 2, this time, working from the outside and moving into the middle. Do the same on the right side, using Thread 3 to tie basic right hand double knots around Threads 1 and 2.

19 Finally, using the left hand outer thread, Thread 4, tie basic left hand double knots around Threads 1, 2 and 3, again moving into the middle. Again, do the same on the right side, using Thread 4 to tie basic right hands knots around Threads 1, 2 and 3.

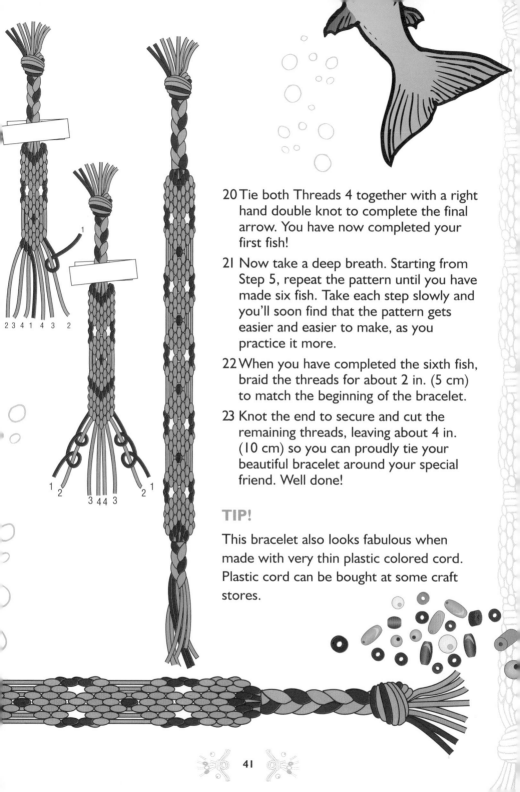

20 Tie both Threads 4 together with a right hand double knot to complete the final arrow. You have now completed your first fish!

21 Now take a deep breath. Starting from Step 5, repeat the pattern until you have made six fish. Take each step slowly and you'll soon find that the pattern gets easier and easier to make, as you practice it more.

22 When you have completed the sixth fish, braid the threads for about 2 in. (5 cm) to match the beginning of the bracelet.

23 Knot the end to secure and cut the remaining threads, leaving about 4 in. (10 cm) so you can proudly tie your beautiful bracelet around your special friend. Well done!

TIP!

This bracelet also looks fabulous when made with very thin plastic colored cord. Plastic cord can be bought at some craft stores.

Novelty Projects

If you have worked your way through the book to this section, you will now be quite an expert at making friendship bracelets. Why not put some of your new-found skills into practice and try making some of the following fun novelty projects? You and your friends are sure to love the results!

Birthday Bracelet

What better time to give your friend a special bracelet than on their birthday? This bracelet uses a variation of the Beaded Braids pattern on Page 22 to create a unique gift your friend will love.

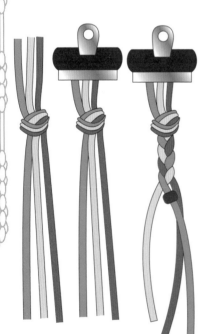

YOU WILL NEED:

- COLORED SILKY CORD, IN THE COLOR OF YOUR FRIEND'S BIRTHSTONE (SEE CHART ON OPPOSITE PAGE) SMALL FANCY BEADS IN THE COLOR OF YOUR FRIEND'S BIRTHSTONE (SEE CHART ON OPPOSITE PAGE)

- TAPE MEASURE

- SCISSORS

- CLIPBOARD, OR OTHER METHOD OF SECURING YOUR CORD FROM PAGE 7

1 Cut three pieces of cord about 36 in. (91 cm) long. Then tie a knot about 4 in. (10 cm) from the top of the cord.

BIRTHSTONE CHART

HERE IS A BIRTHSTONE CHART THAT WILL SHOW YOU WHAT COLOR BEADS TO CHOOSE FOR YOUR FRIEND'S BIRTHDAY FRIENDSHIP BRACELET:

January		Garnet
February		Amethyst
March		Aquamarine
April		Diamond
May		Emerald
June		Pearl, Moonstone
July		Ruby
August		Peridot
September		Sapphire
October		Opal, Tourmaline
November		Yellow Topaz, Citrine
December		Blue Topaz, Turquoise

2 Now clip the cords to the clipboard, or use one of the other methods on Page 7 to keep them firmly in place.

3 Straighten out the three cords so they do not become tangled. Then begin to braid them. Just do two braids, and then add a bead and begin to braid again.

4 One at a time, thread a single bead onto one of the cords, every second time it becomes the left side cord.

5 Continue braiding and adding beads until the bracelet is as long as you like. Then tie a knot to secure and cut the remaining cords, leaving about 4 in. (10 cm) of cord, so you can tie the bracelet onto your friend's wrist. What a cool birthday gift!

Summer Fun

What could be better than hanging out at the beach with your friends in summer, soaking up the sun, playing in the sand and swimming in the waves? You can make your friends a cool friendship bracelet to remind them of those happy times!

YOU WILL NEED:

- BLUE UPHOLSTERY THREAD OR OTHER STRONG THREAD
- SELECTION OF SMALL SHELLS WITH HOLES PIERCED IN THEM (AVAILABLE FROM MOST CRAFT STORES)
- TAPE MEASURE
- SCISSORS
- CLIPBOARD, OR OTHER METHOD OF SECURING YOUR THREADS FROM PAGE 7

1 This bracelet is made with a variation of the Twister pattern on Page 20. First, cut three pieces of thread about 48 in. (122 cm) long. Then fold the threads in half and tie a knot in the top, so you now have six threads.

2 Clip the threads to the clipboard, or use one of the other methods on Page 7 to keep them firmly in place.

3 Now collect all the threads together in a bunch, leaving one thread out (Thread 1 in the diagram).

4 Tie a basic left hand knot with the single Thread 1, around the bunch. Repeat this ten times, making sure the knots are pulled tight towards the left each time.

Thread 1

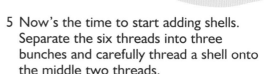

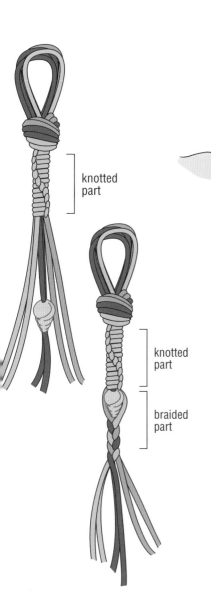

knotted
part

knotted
part

braided
part

5 Now's the time to start adding shells.
   Separate the six threads into three
   bunches and carefully thread a shell onto
   the middle two threads.

6 Braid the three bunches of threads using
   the technique shown in the Simple Braids
   pattern on Page 18, until the braided part
   of the bracelet is as long as the knotted
   part. Then thread another shell onto the
   two middle threads.

7 Collect all the threads together again, but
   leave one thread on the left side out.
   This thread will now be called Thread 1.

8 Repeat Steps 4-7 until the bracelet is as
   long as you like. Then tie a knot to
   secure and cut the remaining threads,
   leaving about 4 in. (10 cm), so you can
   tie the bracelet around your friend's
   wrist. The perfect summer gift!

TIP!

On some beaches, you can collect your
own tiny shells. Ask an adult to pierce
holes in them for you, using a darning
needle.

Happy Halloween

Have fun at Halloween with the super glow-in-the-dark friendship bracelet. You can make one for yourself as well as your friends. Then you can all wear them when you go trick-or-treating!

YOU WILL NEED:

- GLOW-IN-THE-DARK THREAD (AVAILABLE FROM MOST CRAFT STORES)
- REGULAR BLACK COTTON THREAD
- PACKET OF GLOW-IN-THE-DARK BEADS (AVAILABLE FROM MOST CRAFT STORES)
- TAPE MEASURE
- SCISSORS
- CLIPBOARD, OR OTHER METHOD OF SECURING YOUR THREADS FROM PAGE 7

1 This bracelet is made with a variation of the Twin Ties pattern, on Page 16. First, cut three pieces of glow-in-the-dark thread about 36 in. (91 cm) long. Then cut three pieces of black thread, the same length. Then tie a knot about 4 in. (10 cm) from the top of the threads.

2 Now clip the threads to the clipboard, or use one of the other methods on Page 7 to keep them firmly in place.

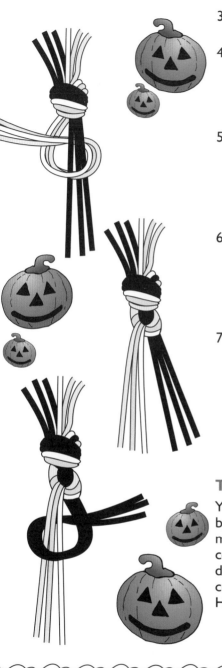

3 Separate the threads, one color to the left and one color to the right.

4 Start with the left three threads and tie a single basic left hand knot around the right three threads. Hold the right threads tight and pull the left threads towards the left.

5 Now take the right three threads (number 2 in the diagram) and tie a single basic right hand knot around the three left hand threads (number 1 in the diagram). Hold the left threads tight and pull the right threads towards the right.

6 Tie another three left and right hand knots, and then carefully thread a glow-in-the-dark bead onto one or two of the glow-in-the-dark threads. Continue tying another three left and right hand knots, then stop and add another bead.

7 Continue tying left and right knots and adding beads until the bracelet is as long as you like. Then tie a knot to secure, and cut the remaining threads. Be sure to leave about 4 in. (10 cm), so you can tie the bracelet around your friend's wrist. Switch off the lights and watch that bracelet glow!

TIP!

You can vary this pattern by adding more threads and more beads. Try different combinations of glow-in-the-dark and regular threads, to create different spooky Halloween looks.

Christmas  Colors

Here's a beautiful Christmas friendship bracelet pattern that you can make for your best friend. It uses a different pattern to those we've shown you previously, but it is quite simple to learn and gives beautiful results!

YOU WILL NEED:

- GREEN AND RED COLORED UPHOLSTERY THREADS, OR THICKER EMBROIDERY FLOSS, SHINY CORD OR WOOLEN YARN
- TAPE MEASURE
- SCISSORS
- CLIPBOARD, OR OTHER METHOD OF SECURING YOUR THREADS FROM PAGE 7

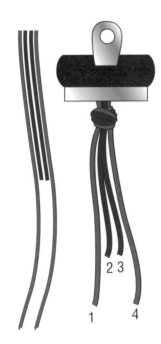

1 Cut two red threads, each about 24 in. (61 cm) long. Then cut two green threads, each about 50 in. (127 cm) long.

2 Tie the threads together with a knot about 2 in. (5 cm) from the top of the threads.

3 Clip the threads to the clipboard, or use one of the other methods on Page 7 to keep them firmly in place. Separate the threads and arrange them in the order shown.

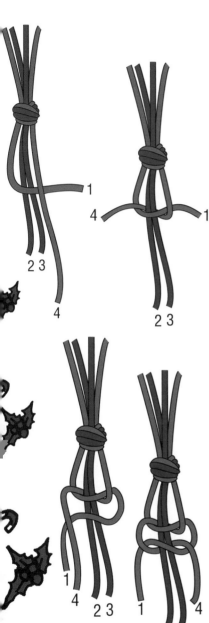

4 Cross Thread 1 over the Threads 2 and 3. Then pass it underneath Thread 4, as shown.

5 Cross Thread 4 underneath Threads 2 and 3. Then pass it over Thread 1, as shown. Pull Threads 1 and 4 to tighten the knot you have made. Thread 1 is now on the right hand side.

6 Cross Thread 1 back over Threads 2 and 3. Then pass it under Thread 4, as shown. Again, cross Thread 4 under Threads 2 and 3, and pass it over Thread 1. Once more, pull Threads 1 and 4 to tighten.

7 Repeat steps 4 to 6 until the bracelet is as long as you want it to be. Then tie a knot to secure and cut the threads, leaving about 4 in. (10 cm) to tie the bracelet around your friend. Gorgeous!

TIP!

You can easily add beads to the bracelet. Just pop a bead on the two center threads after every few knots, for that extra-special look.

Ice Crystals

It may be wintry and cold outside, but this fabulous glittering bracelet will warm your special friend's heart when you give it to them. Try a variety of bead shapes with the bracelet, to give it a unique look. Or use different shaped beads for different friends!

YOU WILL NEED:

- WHITE CORD AND SILVER CORD
- SELECTION OF CLEAR CRYSTAL BEADS (AVAILABLE FROM MOST CRAFT STORES)
- TAPE MEASURE
- SCISSORS
- CLIPBOARD, OR OTHER METHOD OF SECURING YOUR THREADS FROM PAGE 7

1 Once again, this bracelet is made with a variation of the Twister pattern on Page 20. First, cut two pieces of white cord about 48 in. (122 cm) long. Then cut one piece of silver cord the same length. Fold the cords in half and tie a knot in the top, so you now have six cords.

2 Clip the cords to the clipboard, or use one of the other methods on Page 7 to keep them firmly in place.

3 Now collect all the cords together in a bunch, leaving one silver cord out (Cord 1 in the diagram). Tie a basic left hand knot with the single Cord 1, around the bunch. Repeat this ten times, making sure the knots are pulled tight towards the left each time.

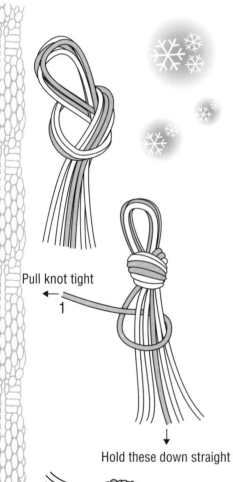

Pull knot tight
← 1

Hold these down straight

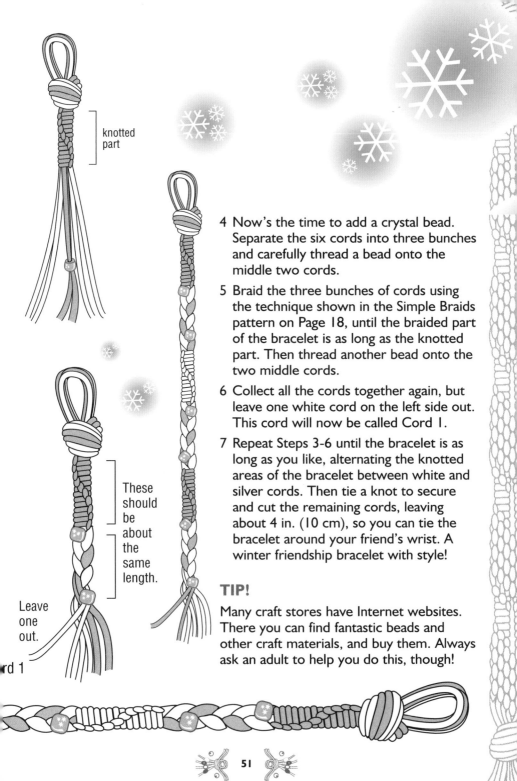

knotted
part

These
should
be
about
the
same
length.

Leave
one
out.

rd 1

4 Now's the time to add a crystal bead. Separate the six cords into three bunches and carefully thread a bead onto the middle two cords.

5 Braid the three bunches of cords using the technique shown in the Simple Braids pattern on Page 18, until the braided part of the bracelet is as long as the knotted part. Then thread another bead onto the two middle cords.

6 Collect all the cords together again, but leave one white cord on the left side out. This cord will now be called Cord 1.

7 Repeat Steps 3-6 until the bracelet is as long as you like, alternating the knotted areas of the bracelet between white and silver cords. Then tie a knot to secure and cut the remaining cords, leaving about 4 in. (10 cm), so you can tie the bracelet around your friend's wrist. A winter friendship bracelet with style!

TIP!

Many craft stores have Internet websites. There you can find fantastic beads and other craft materials, and buy them. Always ask an adult to help you do this, though!

Charming Charms

Charm bracelets are wonderful pieces of jewelry. You can make your friend a special charm friendship bracelet, dripping with unusual sequins and beads!

YOU WILL NEED:

- SHINY SILVER OR GOLD CORD
- A SELECTION OF UNUSUALLY SHAPED BEADS (WE'RE USING ANIMALS)
- ASSORTED SILVER OR GOLD SEQUINS
- SEWING NEEDLE AND SILVER OR GOLD THREAD
- TAPE MEASURE
- SCISSORS
- CLIPBOARD, OR OTHER METHOD OF SECURING YOUR THREADS FROM PAGE 7

1 This bracelet uses the basic Friendship Arrows pattern on Page 24. However, it is more difficult to do because all the cords used are the same color. Make sure you are very good at creating the Friendship Arrows bracelet before you attempt this one!

2 Cut four threads, each about 50 in. (127 cm) long. Now go back to Page 24 and follow the instructions, to complete a Friendship Arrows bracelet.

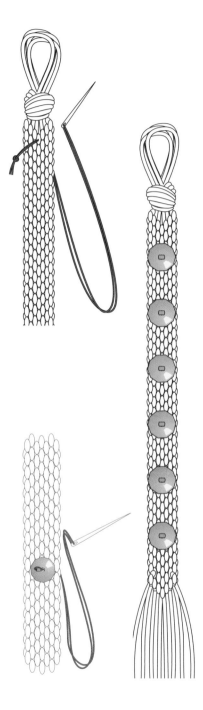

3 Once you have completed your bracelet, you are going to make it extra special by adding your sequins and beads. You might like an adult to help you with the next part, as you need to use a sharp sewing needle.

4 Cut a length of thread, and thread your needle. Then tie a double knot in the thread, to ensure it stays securely on the back of the bracelet.

5 Turn the bracelet over onto what will be the back and make a small stitch, to ensure that the knot and the end of the thread stay in place. Then poke the needle and thread through to the front of the bracelet.

6 Now thread a sequin onto the thread, followed by a bead. Take the thread over the bead and poke it back down the hole in the center of the sequin. Make a few small stitches to hold the bead and sequin in place.

7 Repeat Steps 4-7 another four to six times, until you have decorated your bracelet with the desired number of beads. Then watch your friend's joy when you present them with their charming new bracelet.

TIP!

This bracelet looks great if you attach a clasp and ring to it. Simply thread the cords through the ring at the beginning, when you fold them in half. Then tie a knot, as usual. Then knot the clasp onto the end of your bracelet.

Super Suede

Everyone loves that earthy, casual look. You can make a beautiful, soft brown friendship bracelet with suede cord that will last and last. Your friends will want to wear it for ever!

YOU WILL NEED:

- SEVERAL LENGTHS OF THIN SUEDE CORD (AVAILABLE FROM CRAFT STORES)
- TAPE MEASURE
- SCISSORS
- CLIPBOARD, OR OTHER METHOD OF SECURING YOUR THREADS FROM PAGE 7

1 This bracelet uses the same pattern as the Christmas Colors bracelet, on Page 48. Cut two suede cords, each about 24 in. (61 cm) long. Then cut two more, each about 50 in. (127 cm) long.

2 Tie the cords together with a knot about 2 in. (5 cm) from the top of the threads.

3 Clip the cords to the clipboard, or use one of the other methods on Page 7 to keep them firmly in place. Separate the cords and arrange them in the order shown.

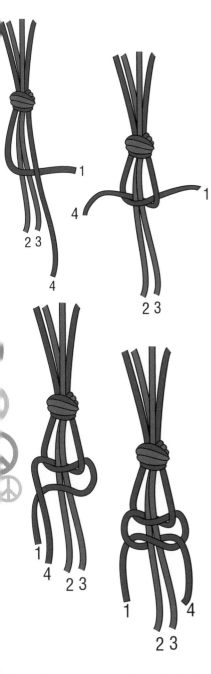

4 Cross Cord 1 over the Cords 2 and 3. Then pass it underneath Cord 4, as shown.

5 Cross Cord 4 underneath Cords 2 and 3. Then pass it over Cord 1, as shown. Pull Cords 1 and 4 to tighten the knot you have made. Cord 1 is now on the right hand side.

6 Cross Cord 1 back over Cords 2 and 3. Then pass it under Cord 4, as shown. Again, cross Cord 4 under Cords 2 and 3, and pass it over Cord 1. Once more, pull Cords 1 and 4 to tighten.

7 Repeat steps 4 to 6 until the bracelet is as long as you want it to be. Then tie a knot to secure and cut the cords, leaving about 4 in. (10 cm) to tie the bracelet around your friend. See how great it looks!

TIP!

This bracelet also looks terrific when made from plain leather cord, string, or hemp. The chunky pattern and earthy style makes a great boys' friendship bracelet, too.

Beaded Flowers

Your friends will be thrilled when you make them one of these delicate friendship bracelets, full of little beaded flowers. This beading technique takes a little practice but you'll soon get the hang of it. Then try creating different floral patterns of your own!

YOU WILL NEED:

- STRONG BROWN UPHOLSTERY THREAD (AVAILABLE FROM CRAFT STORES)
- PINK AND WHITE SMALL PONY BEADS (AVAILABLE FROM CRAFT STORES)
- SMALL JEWELRY JUMP RING AND CLASP (AVAILABLE FROM CRAFT STORES)
- TAPE MEASURE
- SCISSORS

1 First, cut a length of thread 36 in. (91 cm) long. You do not need to secure this to a clipboard, as in previous patterns.

2 Now thread six pink beads onto the thread and position them in the middle of the thread.

3 Take the right hand end of the thread, and bring it back around to the first left hand bead, as shown. Then loop it through and pull all the beads into a tight little circle. These are the petals of the flower.

Push bead towards centre

Pull

4 Thread one white bead onto the left hand thread and push it into the center of the flower. Then push the thread through the right hand bead, as shown. You should now have both threads placed evenly at both sides of the flower.

5 Carefully tie a knot at each side of the flower, to hold it in place.

6 Now thread four white beads onto each side of the flower. Tie another knot to hold the beads in place, then thread four more pink beads. Tie another knot. Continue threading alternately colored beads until your bracelet is the desired length.

7 Cut the threads on each side of the bracelet, leaving about 2 in. (5 cm), and attach the jump ring and clasp to the bracelet, securing them with double knots. Then present the beautiful bracelet to your friend.

TIP!

You can create different colored bracelets for each of your friends. Think about which color would suit them best, and start beading!

Matching Accessories

The knotting, braiding, beading and weaving techniques you have learnt when making friendship bracelets can be used to make your friends other exciting presents. Why not make them some matching accessories? You can give them to your friends at the same time as you give them their bracelets. You can also make a range of accessories for yourself, personalizing them by choosing your favorite bracelet patterns and colors. So what are you waiting for? Start creating!

Necklaces

You can make beautiful long necklaces by using the Basic Braid or Beaded Braid patterns in this book. The Friendship Arrows pattern also makes a beautiful thick choker necklace, too. You can make different necklaces for different occasions, and attach jewelry jump rings and clasps, to make the necklaces easy to take on and off.

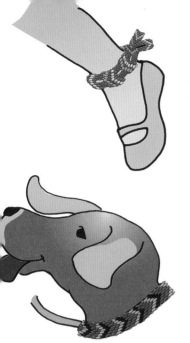

Anklets

Anklets are one of the coolest accessories to wear in summer. They look great when worn with shorts and sandals, or when you're at the beach. All the patterns we've featured in this book make great anklets, but we especially like the Arrows and Twists pattern. When made with upholstery thread, it makes a beautiful, strong anklet.

Pet Collars

Don't leave Fido or Puss out of your Friendship Bracelet fun! Dress them up with beautiful collars that match your own bracelets. At Christmas, try making them a new collar in the Christmas Colors pattern. Make a thicker collar by using colored leather strips, or thick wool. Your gift will make your cute pet look even cuter.

Laces

You can make a whole selection of cool laces for your shoes and sneakers, using the patterns in this book. The Twin Ties pattern makes wonderful chunky laces when done in thick wool or cord. And making laces with the Twister pattern will have everyone staring at your feet in admiration!

Key Chains

Want to jazz up your keys? Or give a friend who keeps losing their keys a useful present? Then add some style by creating a friendship keychain, using strong upholstery thread and one of the patterns from this book.

Ribbons

Got a friend with long hair? Then why not make them some matching friendship ribbons, to go with their friendship bracelet? Buy some very thin ribbon and plait and knot it, just as you do with thread. The end results will look gorgeous.

Your Own Designs

Use these pages to create some of your very own friendship bracelet patterns. Sketch them out and then try making them, using the techniques you have learned in this book.

Your Own Designs

TIP!

You can also find different friendship bracelet patterns on the Internet. Ask an adult to help you find them.

The Friendship Promise

When one friend gives another friend a friendship bracelet, they sometimes make a special pledge or promise, as they tie it on. Here are five examples of a friendship promise that you could make. It's also fun to make up your own special, personal one.

When making up your own promise, think carefully about what you like about your friend. Tell them how much you care!

Like the circle of this bracelet,
Our friendship will never end.
I give this gift to you,
Because you are my friend.

I give this bracelet to you, my friend,
Hoping our friendship will never end.
I promise to be the best friend I can be,
To show how much you mean to me,
I give this bracelet to you, my friend.

I give you this bracelet so you'll see,
Our friendship means so much to me.
As I tie this on, I pledge to you,
That I'll be a friend, forever true.

I made this bracelet with love for you,
Because I am your pal, through and through.
I hope our friendship will never end,
Wear this bracelet with pride, my very best friend.

Friends forever,
Friends for life,
Friends through good times,
Or times of strife.
I give you this bracelet,
So you'll see,
How much our friendship,
Means to me.

Friendship List

To ensure that your friendship bracelets are just perfect for that special someone, you will need to find out some information before you begin making them their gift. To make this easier for you, we have drawn up a table so you can record your information. It will help you to remember who you have made your friendship bracelets for. Just fill in the details and away you go!

RECORDED INFORMATION	FRIEND'S NAME	FRIEND'S NAME	FRIEND'S NAME	FRIEND'S NAME
DATE				
TYPE OF FRIEND				
FAVOURITE COLORS				
LEAST FAVOURITE COLORS				
TYPE OF BRACELET				